Gallery Books
Editor Peter Fallon
RAISED AMONG VULTURES

Molly Twomey

RAISED AMONG VULTURES

Gallery Books

Raised Among Vultures
was first published
simultaneously in paperback
and in a clothbound edition
in 2022.
Reprinted 2022 and 2023.

The Gallery Press
Loughcrew
Oldcastle
County Meath
Ireland

www.gallerypress.com

All rights reserved. For permission
to reprint or broadcast these poems,
write to The Gallery Press:
books@gallerypress.com

© Molly Twomey 2022

The right of Molly Twomey to be identified as Author of this Work has been asserted in accordance with Section 77 of the Copyright, Designs and Patents Act 1988.

ISBN 978 1 91133 839 0 *paperback*
     978 1 91133 840 6 *clothbound*

A CIP catalogue record for this book
is available from the British Library.

Raised Among Vultures receives financial assistance from the Arts Council.

Contents

Risk *page* 11
The Drop Off 12
Heirlooms 13
Injury 14
Tread Lightly 15
Babysitter 16
The Most Brutal Thing 17
Tumblr 18
Acorns 19
Chips 20
Gráinne 21
Noah's Wife 22
Midas 23
Forget-me-nots 24
Sister's Keeper 25
As Light 26
Samhain 27
Wildfire 28
Acupuncture 29
Strawberry Moon 30
Dead Ends 31
Zipping Up My Mother's Dress 32
Crumbling 34
Online Group Therapy 36
Knives We Used on Our Skin 37
Echo 38
Notebook 39
Everyone here is dead honest . . . 40
Wednesdays, Half-five 41
Au Pair in Marseille 42
Tiny and Compact 43
Massage 44
Nightshade 45
Relay to Thin 46
Under Your Skin 48

Don't pick me tulips . . . 49
Philomel 50
Bluebeard 51
Caught Dead 52
I did not eat for three weeks . . . 53
Liz's Kitchen 54
Waking 55
Famine Walls 56
A Sleepless Mind 57
Pipistrelles 58
Splint 59
Hurlers 60
The Secret Zips 61
I Teach My Brother How to Disappear 63
Reverse 64
Twenty-one Questions 65
Baggage 66
Attendance Award 67
Marathon 68
All the Things I Want to Do 69
Mantras 70
Hiding 71
Kinsale 72

Acknowledgements and Notes 74

*for everyone who has loved and
supported me along the way*

Risk

All I want is to be shot
        into the air by a starship,

thrown far from waiting rooms, gurneys
        and supervised toilet trips;

a pill punched from its dispenser.
        I get it, she says,

interrupting my list of amusement parks
        I'll visit when I'm discharged.

She drags her scarlet nail along her sternum,
        says, *I love the thrill*

that a belt might loosen, a spring could snap.
        She shows me how to hide

supplements in a cactus pot,
        to raid the contraband cabinet

when the nurse who falls asleep is on.
        Can you feel it? she asks, placing my palm

on her chest, hers on mine.
        The bumper cars of our hearts stutter and jolt.

The Drop Off

Everything's a blur. You don't play Talking Heads,
Bob Dylan, talk about work or your iffy stomach.

You read the road as if it's encrypted
with what a father should say on a drive like this.

Should I apologize for your missed appointments,
unread emails? There is always someone

who needs you more. Mostly I'm sorry
that I'm not as happy as you raised me to be.

I want to ask the GPS the quickest route to end this silence.
When we reach The Centre you pull up and go straight

for the boot. This is what you know to do,
to lift the heavy thing, tell me to take your good umbrella.

You drag my suitcase to the door where the nurse stands
with a notepad and clutches your arm.

I'll come back soon, you say,
but she smiles and says, *It's better if you don't.*

Heirlooms

My dietician says if I don't eat
my oestrogen won't restore.
My body will always be a door

locked on its hinges,
safe-guarding its room
of dust and secrets.

Her toddler behind her scribbles
as if his life depends on it.
Is he heavy enough that she could use him

as a kettlebell for Russian twists?
A dumbbell for deadlifts?
I shake off my thoughts

and ask if eating disorders are genetic,
if I will pass on this loss
of bone mass and conscience.

Injury

I drag it like roadkill up Shandon Street,
down Turner's Cross, my snapped tendon,
my inflamed arch. You suggest we pause,

stretch, go again. I tell you between breaths
that *if I don't run for exactly sixty minutes
I'll sprint into the Lee*; the moon,

a searchlight on wounded skin.
When's the last time you felt that way? you ask.
A year since I was found on Gaol Bridge.

Your patience is the chewed flesh inside my cheek
as I refuse to stop for traffic lights
or to thumb a gnat from your cornea.

You tell me that exercise is the last thing
my disorder controls, that right now I am somewhere,
someone else. You almost reach for my arm, but don't.

Tread Lightly

On our run you give me a wide berth,
aware I am trying to outsprint
his voice, tear his tracker from my wrist.

For so long I thought it was romantic to have him hold me
up by the throat, to let him knife through my wardrobe,
gift me baggy sweaters, oversized shirts.

My mouth was a touch screen
unlocked only for him,
my flesh, the punched-in foil on a pack of pills.

You tread lightly, conscious of how easily I flinch,
your breath quiet and consistent as sunlight,
the tiny bloom of muscle under skin.

Babysitter

When I was swapping Coco Pops
for low-fat cottage cheese,

saving up for an ab belt
and pleading with God to sculpt me thin,

my babysitter showed me
an ad on TV of children

with swollen abdomens and fruit flies
in the corners of their crusting lips.

These kids, she said, *would give anything
for the chicken dippers under your plate,*

the Penguin bar tucked up your sleeve.
After that everything tasted like guilt

but still I gripped the trophy of my ribs,
refused each sugared drink.

She was the first to see what I was becoming
and not praise me for it.

The Most Brutal Thing

Mother 'threw anorexic daughter's body into the sea'.

The papers called her insane,
    a nurse who spent her life in waiting rooms

as her child was fastened and refastened to a gurney,
    a gastric tube stuck to her face.

She could cure a stranger's rash,
    steam out a flu but she could not stop

her daughter folding in on herself
    like an origami fortune.

She kept Katerina's heart and shrivelled kidneys
    for nine whole days

before letting her drift jelly-brained and weightless
    over a cardiogram of waves.

The police reported no evidence
    of violent death, but isn't starving yourself

the most brutal thing? The slow collapse
    of bones, sprained ankles to sunken cheeks,

the last segment of voice
    burrowing into muffled quiet.

Tumblr

I was preparing for an apocalypse of bone,
under the stairs in that currach-dark.
I saved pictures of ribs and clavicles in monochrome,

the way Noah's wife gathered figs and dried plums.
She too did not have a name
like SkinnyGirlSixteen, ProAna98.

Our messages fluttered onto each other's screens;
we confessed skinned apples, Diet Cokes,
prescribed black coffee, three thousand sit-ups.

I did not have a device of my own
so sat each night deleting laced wrists and pearled spines
from my family's files of Christmas quizzes,

recipes and maps of hikes. I shook the modem
to get it to work, witnessed those photos tumble
into the tiny grey trash can, bone by bone.

Acorns

And after
I have whittled my flesh
down to bone

my body grows fur like a red squirrel,
in the claws of autumn,
collecting acorns.

Chips

We wait for our chips to be seared in oil,
onion rings battered in fat.
I don't know how to tell him that I haven't eaten

grease in five years, that I still dab ten grams
of melted cheddar with a napkin,
that the torrential hiss of mackerel,

squish of mustard between bun and burger,
makes me want to run suicide drills in a blender
of wind. Before I can speak my date slips

his coat over my arms;
my wrists ease into his deep pockets.
Buried there, a wish stone,

small and compact in my palm.
The years it spent under the tidal tug and thrash,
hardening grain, hoarding bone.

Gráinne

Everything struck fear,
a deer's hooves

could be a man's boots,
a glow-worm, a torch.

They pasted our faces
to poles, notice boards,

called us animals
who ransacked the ark,

our sins denounced
in small kitchens.

We chewed 'shrooms,
pitched my wedding dress as a tent.

I lay in the church of his hands
and dragonflies stitched the air

like monks weaving prayers.
God was in the tulips

loosening their pent-up bulbs.
Let it be known that we were loved.

Noah's Wife

We hadn't touched in years. All he did was tinker
in the shed, mutter to himself.

I'll admit when the first rain hit I ran
onto the boat with the ram and the goat,
feared the vixen's teeth, the antlers of the moose.

Noah was glued to the wheel so I set a truce:
I wouldn't salt the flank of a cow
or rip the leg off a goose

if the buffalo kept its horns to itself
and the snake flattened to a belt.

I slept with my head on the stomach of an ox.
We shared dried apricots and fermented malt.

When our ship pulled in an olive dropped
from the dove's lips, deer flinched,
the ape turned away. They ran, crawled, sniffed

and leapt into the sea. As if they knew our pact
wouldn't last, like the rainbow in the sky,
my husband's hand hovering over mine.

Midas

Over a dark slab of beef hiding mouldering chips
he unseals another rejection,

paces back and forth. Was it the gaps on his CV?
His limp grip of the manager's hand?

The way a child shrinks to be whacked with a belt
he crouches by the fireplace,

holds out his slack fingers, useless wrists.
The fire cracks and spits; he dangles his life-

lines over it, winces as blood pickles under his skin.
If he were man enough he'd have a mortgage, job, kids.

Instead, alone, he watches his flesh blister and melt off
his carpal bones, dead stars bursting into molten gold.

Forget-me-nots

You stick up a note saying DO NOT DISTURB,
the way forget-me-nots, empty of nectar,
fade their inner rings so bumblebees and graylings

leave them alone. I burst through your hospital door,
feed you grapes you can no longer swallow.
When the nurse comes we speak over you,

hornets pretending not to see the stalk
of your sternum. In the halls she probes,
Where is his mother? Why is it always only me?

You will not let me call her and I'll never let you sleep
past nine or look at any screen
for more than twenty-five minutes. You want me to go

back to your flat, to eat stale tofu and water the plants.
You were so slow to say you loved me,
as if it's selfish to love when you're ill.

But my prayer beads cling to your guard rails,
your flora swims in my gut. I kiss your lymph-coloured
skin and whisper, *I'll be back tomorrow.*

Sister's Keeper

We don't talk about your hair loss,
your skull like a stepping stone eaten by lichen,
or the tubes that tether you to the bed

in the room where we used to watch TV.
Instead, on a day your pain is a 3,
we go to see *My Sister's Keeper*, rated 13.

We swap fake birth years for red velvet seats.
I don't hear the girl's screams
as her brows and lashes fall out,

but the sniffles trapped in your nose
and that growing kernel of hurt in your throat.
You don't laugh when the girl reads a cancer

horoscope as a joke but quietly slurp a Coke
like a huge cup of starless sky and, my God,
I want so badly to hold you, to say,

It'll be alright, but what do I know
with my cookie dough, my fizzy lemon?
An attendant blocks the screen

to cut our tiny yellow ticket stubs.
He shines a torch on your toes that barely touch
the floor like the sun we stumble into,

expecting only dark and the pale crescent shape
bones make when they're tucked up
in the living room after the everlasting day.

As Light

My mother finds a pale white feather
and palms her chest. Her eyelids fall
like the light cotton of prayer flags in Tibet.

For years she pulled locks of my hair
like dead wrens cleaving
to pillows, nesting in clothes.

She held worry like a worm in her throat
as she handed me over to GPs,
therapists, DXA scans and ECGs.

She lays the feather on the windowsill,
messy and soft as the new growth
at my occipital bone.

Samhain

My mother lays a pumpkin on my black hospital tray.
She knows I cannot bob for apples, snap a Twix

without wanting to throw myself off the pier.
I cut its skull, scrape the rind clean. She tells me

in the past women used to place embers in beets
to ward off evil spirits. Meaning she wants to reach

into my bone cage, drag out the creature that bangs
its hollow cup inside me. I want to hold her,

tell her it will be okay, but my body has shrunk
so tiny if she touches me she will break.

I wipe the inner walls with bleach.
Sometimes I wish the nurse would lay a hand

on Mam's wrist, whisper I am not her daughter,
there was some mistake. But only the receptionist

calls in to warn visiting times are over.
My mother picks up her purse and smooths her jeans.

Later she tells me she found crushed eggshells
and albumen smeared on her windscreen.

She drove though she could not see and kept asking God,
Why me? I carve a mouth, beg it to speak.

Wildfire

The radio says it took three days to ease the flames
on the heather and gorse in my mother's favourite

quilt of land. It's likely that a wanderer threw a match
at the moor and walked away. The sun's hardly up

and Mam chops turnips, leeks and shallots,
pulls the stem off a radish, a red grenade in the heart-

lines of her palms. She swigs a glass of wine and *click-
click-click*s the gas, adds more and more oil, tips a bowl

of eggplant. I don't know who she's trying to feed.
She empties the whole fridge and hums

as the pan splatters its magma, laughs
into the fresh welts in her hands. I try not to look

away. Stonechats and merlins have lost their homes,
sikas cannot hide from hunters. I read once that the word

melt-down comes from burning metal. How tough
my mother is. How much the world has burnt her.

Acupuncture

Mam holds a needle
over my navel,
aims for my CV12.

She squints
as when she used to repair
my school skirt hem.

This is the sixth steel tip
she presses into my raw-
boned stomach.

It bends and snaps.
She will never stop trying
to stitch me back.

Strawberry Moon

Before my father sold me
he fed me crystals and our jaws
danced with each other.

We placed our ears to the floorboards,
listened to the growl of jaguars
and chased geckos up the walls.

The tamer who bought me
thirsted to lick my diamond-
crusted lips and made my father rich.

Dad knew I would return
like the moon that looks strawberry
but can be Beaver, Buck and Full Wolf.

Dead Ends

Mam would never collect me
from the nightclub. She liked to drop me off,
marvel at sparkly legs, ringlets neat

as napkinned cutlery. Mostly my mother loved
her chamomile tea, lavender bed sheet.
She never saw broken shards

of Heineken bottles in my cheek,
screaming matches at the chip van
where tyres got slashed and taxis refused

to take me and my friends in their leatherette seats.
We sang by the pier with our bare ankles dangling
over the 16-foot drop I once dragged my ex-love from

like a rusted blade from the back of my wardrobe.
I always slept on someone else's floor,
clogged their carpet with my peach vodka breath

and stole six slices of white bread,
returned to my mother light as a china cup,
with her Sunday papers, yoghurt and mango.

Had I asked her to come for me
on those nights, in her '94 Volvo Estate
like a hearse when most of the blood

I wore was not my own,
surely it would have eased the shock
when she found my limbs bare and shivering.

She could not coax me from the dark,
hold to her heart what was left of my body,
stem of a snapped wine glass.

Zipping Up My Mother's Dress

Her hands church her midriff.
It's a ten, she says, *I can't believe it fits*.
She's been eating raw carrots, counting her steps.

What does she want me to say?
That I'm glad she's smaller? That she looks great?
She used to be a tight twelve.

That extra flesh was the decade
she banned diet books,
snacked on almond pastries

and drove me to dieticians and therapists.
We revved past joggers,
turned up the heat, thanked Christ

I stopped getting up to sprint.
At the pharmacy she waded me through
carb blockers and keto shakes.

I'm trying to accept that her body is hers,
not a fire blanket I step on to escape
the flames of my worst years.

Still, how can almost losing me not be enough to kill
her desire to be small? Has she forgotten
the ECGs, the blood tests?

Before I speak
her arms slide around my hips.
She says she's glad that we can shop again,

that she can touch me and I don't flinch.
Her heart against mine, the contraction and release
of a stress toy. She pinches her belly,

asks will she get away with this?
I say, *Yes, I'm buying*, and tear off the tag
so she never knows the price.

Crumbling

The receptionist glares at Áine's
streak of snot on your sleeve.
You get no hotel welcome pack,
no map of the city. Her eyes roll

at your council bag of coins and notes.
She counts them three times,
swipes her counterfeit pen.
Áine is dragging you now,

wants her animal crackers
in the bottom of the case,
the case that holds your life.
She is crying, stomping, shrieking,

you can't sign the document,
Jesus Christ. The receptionist thinks
you can't handle your child.
You yell at her, plead with her.

She doesn't know what it's like
to change a nappy on the side
of the road, to eat dry Rice
Krispies for lunch, to spit blood

'cause you can't afford a toothbrush.
All you want is a table and chairs
so Áine can dip crunchy soldiers
in boiled eggs; heaters to hang

damp socks on and a shower
to clean city grease off your skin;
a bed with fresh linen to sleep
and sleep until you can't remember

the guard who kicked you off the steps
of the church, the woman who held
her purse a little tighter
and the receptionist *tut-tut-tutting*.

Online Group Therapy

He can't leave his house, his flesh an open wound,
air a saline gust. He's been considering meditation

but says it's feminine, weak. I tell him the Navy Seals
practise 'Box Breathing', imagine their sighs

departing in steel containers forklifted from ships.
It's not as if *he*'s climbed an oil rig, taken

someone's life with a sniper rifle. But he's tired
of forcing himself to rise, a sun that drags

its untouched body up to look down at tree stumps
and rubbish trucks. I ask has he heard

of vision boards? Sticking pictures on an A3 card
of what he wants his life to be. *Steve Harvey*, I say,

hangs them in his gym. Mine is all wild mountain
swimming in the Calanques, *café con leche* in Seville

and a drawing of a guy's back — I always choose
a love that turns away from me. This man of forty-four

years with an engineering degree pencils himself
brushing his teeth, clipping his nails, combing

dried black-bean sauce from his beard. He holds it up,
his wet and crusty eyes widening, *Oh Christ*, he says,

I'm so sorry, it's so bad — his tiny selves
without colour or flesh trapped between his fingertips.

Knives We Used on Our Skin

Who did we imagine would pick up our filters,
our shattered glass? Our minds were closed buds.

In the oaks and pines by the old icehouse
we sparked firelighters, threw back naggins,

cans of cherry cider. We sucked Bensons
and mints, had our first kiss, our last smoke.

What did we know of a beer cap in a vixen's throat
or the stomach of a hare gagged with cigarette butts?

All we knew for sure was if we drank enough
we could voice the panic attacks we had before maths,

the mantras that our bodies were too big, too small,
too riddled with spots. We confessed

that we watched our mothers dice carrots
with the knives we used on our skin and babysat kids

by the river we dreamt of walking into.
Here we uncapped what was held so tightly

like a sluice trap after so many winters.
Our tense jaws, our cramped hearts, were held

by the earth's nerves, those roots and vines
that quietly lowered the pressure of our blood.

Echo

I chase you through the train station,
carrying your dead skin and smell of cigarettes.

I beg you to stop. You gaze straight ahead
to the engine's low rev, the crows peck at each other

like wind-battered dulse. And though your shoulders
are stiff tyres and your jaw is rigid as a platform

you must wait for the doors to sync open
their scorpion claws, to unfold your ticket,

and settle into the discomfort of leftover body heat,
how the past always gets in the way of things.

But once I reach your hair like flares that pour out
of your beanie hat you are shorter than before,

and you would never wear those orange shoes,
slurp a sugared latte, or laugh where someone might hear

your gentle boyhood. And even in my new life
where I am blown open again and again by such small beauty,

a wren's chirp, a purple orchid like a woman's bruised hand
reaching through dirt. There is always this scab of your name

on my lips and part of me crawling in the dark,
asking, *Why don't you love me?,* only for the dust-gagged air

to carry my voice back to my own wrung hands
and cut knees, begging, *Why don't you love me?*

Notebook

I find a syringe in his guitar case, drag him to NA,
scrape grime off his sheets, sell my car

to pay his therapist. Nothing kills me more
than his No. 1 hit blasting in A&E

and the radiologist taking a selfie
as he chokes on his vomit. God take me back

to when gin and 7UP, a few of the lads
nodding to his demos, was enough.

I used to dream he'd fill marquees and stadiums.
Now a nurse stuffs a tube through his lips to pump up

acid, pus, black grit. I'd swallow it to have back
the boy with a notebook of songs in his pocket.

Everyone here is dead honest,

no fake smiles, no *Let's meet for coffee.*
Nobody hugs me with their fleshy body
or makes silly faces with their fruit.

We roar when we are hungry,
suck each other's marrow.
Last week we got matching tattoos:

skulls and arrows. We stay up all night,
flossing with each other's veins.
Who knew there were so many ways to die?

Forget sepsis, stroke, malaria —
think swallowing a knife. It isn't that I crave
the crack of my own neck

but I don't want to wake up
and weigh a cup of kale twenty-seven times,
water down my slimline.

Wednesdays, Half-five

Over coffee I tell you I slept with some guy.
You say it's strange I'm okay with touch.
I reply I was drunk, forgetting your dad

who you don't talk about but found
mangled and sallow as turmeric
on the kitchen tiles. You were four.

Instead you gloat about women you find online,
how you pee on their stomachs. When I don't react
you say, *Isn't there something erotic about urine?*

You might take one of them to Brazil for a week,
buy nine of the same watch because you like
how they tick and tattoo your entire arm

black, darkness swallowing you, limb by limb.
I explain my panic attack at the Quay Co-Op,
everything gluten-free, plant-based, organic.

I've been trying to learn there's nothing wrong
with oats or wheat. You joke we should share a scone,
wait for my shoulders to stiffen and fingers to tremble.

I confess I'm jealous of the clavicle that juts
from my granny's chest, the gap between my cousin's legs
under her Communion dress. You nod. You get that.

We ignore the ghosts on our backs, Tara who left
for St Pat's, Jack with *Ogham* script on his wrists,
promise to meet, same time, same place.

Au Pair in Marseille

I always walk in on my host dad naked
        in the kitchen. Nightly

the cat crawls up my stomach,
        presses its claws into my throat.

You show me how to take a pistachio
        from its shell without cracking it open,

like how I will slip from my host dad's back door
        with my passport, my salt-wet cheeks,

move into yours with your spice rack,
        your seven types of tea. We plan movies

and night jogs, ignorant of the danger
        of the dock after dark, the man crouched

in the shadows like a jack-in-the-box.
        In another world our lives go on forever

like this, me setting placemats
        as you roast sweet potato, red peppers, aubergine.

Your lips stay within their perfect skin,
        my blood doesn't pool into your cardigan.

Tiny and Compact

i.m. Nikki Grahame

Hunger in French is *faim* like the fame
she ditched in London when she sold her flat,
grew out her bleached roots.

She worked in a café on *Promenade des Anglais*,
perfected her latte foam art, made stars,
kittens, hearts. The only mirror she owned,

tiny and compact in the bottom of her tote bag.
She sent her therapist a postcard,
told him he was right, she'd never recover

where she got sick. But *faim* is pronounced
less like fame, more like family.
She would always return to the tiny clothes

that groped her wrists, the bed she faked
a bellyache in. A light-up mirror tilted
towards the floor, permanently disappointed in her.

Massage

She switches on the CD and soaks her fingers in rapeseed oil. He removes his shirt and lies on the table. She dims the lights. Applying pressure to his sacrum, her hips move to the motion of her shoulders. She closes her eyes, imagines kneading dough for her two boys, their gapped smiles, runny noses.

    The man grunts and she is back. She moves up to his lungs and presses in, as if he is a bottle of ketchup. He wheezes as she compresses. She wants to squeeze until he can no longer breathe, wants his organs to come out his lips. She will hang them in her hostel like ornaments. He slaps her thigh to say, *That's enough*. And she returns to this man, the clock on the wall, the life she was told to run towards.

Nightshade

She and I circle her apartment block, a cloister.
She's terrified to drink tap water,
to rub moisturizer into her skin.

Sometimes she burns
the whorls on her fingertips,
wonders what it's like to not exist.

I tell her about colouring books,
how making a whale pink, a blackbird yellow,
can give the illusion she could change things.

Do this in the morning, I say,
under the penlight of sun,
mainly to give her a reason to wake.

I show her the relief of ripping up black nightshade,
hurling rotten eggs against cement,
how destroying something might distract her

from how much she wants to hurt herself.
All of this is to say that nobody will help
until she has climbed down

the BMI scale into a comatose state.
I share with her the risks I took
to be thin and cared for.

Relay to Thin

I will never miss seeing my name
    over a hospital postcode.

The letters you wrote about your mother
    who joked, *Isn't it a relief*

you *never wanted to be slim?*
    You knew I hated visitors to the ward,

didn't want anyone to see
    the curly straws of IV fluid,

games of hide-and-seek I played
    with my food. You sent pictures

of us as kids, bandanas knotted
    like pinkie promises at our napes,

rang about the boys who called
    your legs thunder, the age-13 jeans

you'd die to fit your 18-year-old waist in.
    You understood why I held a blade

to my adipose, cut until I was drop-dead
    gorgeous. Now we meet for lunch

in a café, your breastbone juts out of your skin,
    a baton I threw you in this relay.

Thank God, you say, *the chicken isn't fried*
    and peel white flesh into tiny bites.

I want to ask if you're sleeping. When you lie
    on your side do your kneecaps grate,

do you shiver in three sweaters and a duvet?
    I say nothing, knowing your mind

will hear a compliment in a warning.
    I stare at the air between your legs,

your barely-there wrists,
    pinch the gut I'm trying to be okay with.

Under Your Skin

I was sixteen when I felt you kick, tried hangers,
scalding water, the spoke of a bicycle wheel.

You shrieked, howled, wept in that tooth-marked cot,
your tremors rattling the bars. I told mothers

at the playground that I was a sitter,
postmen that my husband would be home later.

At dusk I'd play the video of your birth
in reverse, blood and afterbirth filling me up again.

Once I left you on the steps of the church,
ran back three minutes later, convinced

there were bruises like berries squished
under your skin. I wanted some physical thing

to hate myself for. At twelve you pierced
your navel with a safety pin. My fingers itched

to wring your throat but wiped that seed of blood.
Now, as I gut your room for drugs, I find job specs, CVs,

a photo on your dresser of us on the swings,
me pushing you away and pulling you back in.

Don't pick me tulips,

compare hips to moons,
pluck me concertos
or use the word muse.

My eyes are not periwinkles,
my skin is not linen.

If you try to rub my feet
I'll snap you in half
like the wishbone of a chicken.

There'll be no late nights,
no rubbing shoulders in bed —

if you so much as unbutton
a sleeve without asking
I'll yank you by the scruff of your neck.

Forget bolognese, candles, red wine.
Look, if we are going to do this,
know that I was raised among vultures.

Philomel

Deep in the sundews,
his nails are talons
ripping my skirt,
bruising my hips.

I scream for my sister,
for God, for death.
He calls me a headache,
hot if I wasn't so shrill,

and leaves me there,
tongue-tied, stoned-in,
his damp breath
a tapestry on my neck.

Bluebeard

She doesn't mean to look at his phone
but he's always whispering into it like a Ouija board,
leaves it unlocked on her pillow.

As if he wants her to see the bare chests
of so many ex-girlfriends, their tummies sucked in,
ribs like fingers clawing out of his screen.

She wants to drag them from his group chats,
his devil emojis. How can she ever admit
to finding this? He returns, sparks pixels of tobacco

and coils around her waist, holds her so tightly,
as if trying to shrink her, bury her
in his obituaries of eyes, lips, cleavage.

Caught Dead

I wish I could get mad at you for the empty milk
in the fridge, tripping over your trainers
the third time this week.

Our house doesn't smell like Lynx.
It's full of dried-up tissues like the apple cores
I picked from your sheets. You'd cringe

at all the times you've been called *beautiful*.
Are you worn out from running around
everyone's thoughts and prayers?

There's a minute's silence
at the GAA pitch, as if you'd be caught dead
with a hurley. If you've signal up there

I'll text you the results of the Premier League.
If TNT delivers I'll send a pack of Extra Mints.
God knows you don't deserve it.

I took a five-hour flight, a three-hour train
in this itchy black dress only to fall
over your gym vest, dumbbells, my bedroom

carpet swamped in your sweat. Listen,
I'm coming to the graveyard with a spade,
kicking you out. I'm taking your place.

I did not eat for three weeks

because rent was due and the price of bread
   went up 5 cents
because ghrelin distracted me from you
because two years ago over 100,000 starved in Yemen
   but famine means 1847
because a baby seagull died on my roof
because anti-depressants cause weight gain
because I failed my driving test
   and wanted to achieve something
because you asked if I hated my stomach so much
   why did I wear tight shirts
because sometimes my gag reflex didn't work
because even the driving instructor stood me up
because a woman pushed a buggy
   ten kilometres to Cork Penny Dinners
because I didn't want children
   but needed a physical reason
because when I was eating a cracker
   you joked I was storing for winter
because bones became language
   and my tongue was hole-punched
because you got a tattoo saying, *May the bridges I burn*
   light the way and I was the bridge
because I was not old enough to vote but wanted change

Liz's Kitchen

Why did you become vegan?
To avoid Battenberg on my birthday,
a leg of turkey at Christmas.

But I say,
*I can't remember
what a ladybird looks like.*

She adds so much butter
to her toast, glides the knife
along her tongue,

says she had a daughter like me,
watched her run laps of the lough
with a fractured hip,

found fists of her hair
in the washing machine,
a tooth in the sink.

Here, she throws me her phone,
a red ladybird
like a clot of blood.

Waking

My tongue is a slug
in salt. Is that
my blood on his mattress?

He laughs.
Babe, you are so fucked up.

Can't find my underwear,
      my socks,
don't know
      what street
I'm on. My whole body
      throbs

like a bleeding gum
after a last baby tooth
is ripped out
and dumped.

Famine Walls

The week your husband moves to St Enda's Ward
with motor neuron disease we climb the Knockmealdowns.
Six years ago he was given three winters to live.

You are light with talk about the walls starved cottiers
built for a penny a day. Later I learn each word they had
for stone, *cloch*, *gallán*, *spalla*, *carball*. We sit and peel

blood oranges by the ridge that never sheltered them.
It was too cold and far to walk home so they slept
like the segments of a fruit, curled into each other

on the moor of heather and moss, their flesh eaten
raw by wind. Your sons who will not clean
their father's mower or lift his shears are laying gravel,

six inches deep, on the backyard he used to cut and trim:
the way a repetitive act makes a person feel in control.

It's a miracle, you say, *that rocks last this long*,
a backbone through the strain of so many storms.

A Sleepless Mind

She tweets that she's sick. I go to bed for a week,
zoom in on her selfies, her dirt-less pores.

She knits octopi for premature babies,
ties scarves to oaks for anyone who blisters

in the cold. I dig out my crochet kit
but everything I stitch unravels like a sleepless mind.

I wish I could buy her scent online,
train my tongue to her voice. I cut her bangs

into my hair, my fingertips weaving her tea cosies.
Touch ID no longer recognizes me.

The wind ruffles my fringe back into a crease.
I copy her acai bowl, her lactose allergies,

refresh her feed again and again;
the eye of a needle hooked to her thread.

Pipistrelles

God, I wish I could screech that I want to stop living
in that college flat where leeches of fat slurp

the oven's glass. Leaning against the bridge,
I watch a bat suck a centipede like a jelly worm

around my housemate's tongue as she asks
how I've got so thin. Lately I feel too big

in every room. A pup can weigh a third
of its mother and cut through her skin.

It's impossible to live without breaking someone.
In black clothes I cover the fetid scab of my body.

Only bats know the gnaw of my flesh,
click of bones, pulsing and hidden as eardrums.

Splint

My brother used to enfold himself in the oak
with *Beano* magazines, a can of Coke.

Hidden in leaves like the Toxic Waste sweets
he sucked and spat out in wads of kitchen roll.

Lately he only eats chicken wings, turkey breasts,
gulps raw eggs and protein shakes.

Every day he wraps a resistance band
around his stomach, ties himself to the bole and sprints.

I want to tell him that I too have made wood
of my body, carved it into a coat rack under jackets

of men I thought I loved, a dumb quiet stick.
He is trying to protect the small boy who lived

before the refused engagement ring and unfinished lease.
He can't hear my small voice calling out for him.

Hurlers

Our love notes scrunch up
in their pockets,

we shiver in our wet socks,
grey skirts

at the side of the pitch
as they drill

and pass the *sliotar*
like the world between their fingers.

The Secret Zips

When my brother starts dating a girl I wink,
tell him I saw her walking her collie

by the pier, dipping her feet into ice-cold river.
How does she brave it? He ignores me,

burrows into his phone. Now that their IDs
are no longer in Comic Sans and their birth years

are real I want to take them out for cocktails.
I've always wanted a sister, someone

to weave daisy-chains with, to paint swirls
on our nails. On my lunch break I overhear

two women talk about *gardaí* interviews,
a nightclub and that verb *rape* spat out

in coffee dregs under her sweet, milky name.
It dawns on me that my brother,

whom I can't unsee reading a *Ben 10* magazine
like a bible, is not her boyfriend

but the guy staying up to answer her texts,
to distract her at the aquarium, the cinema,

the hurling pitch. I want to protect him from
the broken glass and held-back hair of the world.

I text him, *I'm so proud of the man you're becoming*.
He replies, *Did something happen? I'm hungry,*

get me something. I grab him a Fanta, a butterfly
cake, almost buy him a pack of the soccer cards

he used to collage. When I was his age my friends
and I lived on Benson cigarettes and instant coffee,

got up before dusk to study we cared so much
about results, our problems tucked like winged pads

in the secret zips of our bags. It was easier
to huddle up at our desks, Tipp-Ex the nights

spent drunk with boys we could barely remember,
would never forget. The air spritzed

with silence — the things we didn't speak,
heavy and clinging like fake tan to our wrists.

I Teach My Brother How to Disappear

What was it like for him, to see me, his sister,
push away a bowl of honeyed Cheerios

for dry spinach leaves, sprinting laps of the garden?
Swapping crayoned heights on the back door

for black lines on the bathroom scales, tracking pounds
to lose with a jar of marbles I used to flick and roll?

My body like his raptor bath-toy that shrank
and clogged the drain, made our parents cross

and loud as bellyache. Lately any time he's sick or 'full'
I'm scared I've taught him to refuse a bag of crisps

or a bar of Milky Way. How could he learn to listen
to his body as I hurled mine against the thin wall

between our rooms, our worlds? The only trick
I showed him was to disappear

but he's still here on the soccer pitch, scoring
a hat-trick in his studded boots, his guarded shins.

Reverse

i.m. Geraldine and Louise Clancy

At 25 my mother teaches me to drive.
Every time I click the seatbelt,

grip the gears, I imagine backing up
to that flooded dyke

on the road between Ballyduff, Kilworth, Fermoy,
to overturn your Ford and coax out

your mother's body, yours,
so you and she could bicker like us,

learning to reverse
in a backyard of docks, clover and moss.

Twenty-one Questions

Have you ever lied to me? I ask. You reply
that, on our fifth date, you said a rock hit the wheel

but it was a chaffinch. You didn't turn and hand me
that small flame of news but drove into the mango

and gunpowder sunset, afraid I'd make you pull up
to check that there were no quavers stuck

in its throat, that if its pulse didn't react to my fingers
tap-dancing on its keel bone I'd want to bury it

under heather and moss. You thought that I'd make you
pray every time we drove from Lismore to Ballynoe,

that our date would become not the boardwalk,
chips and the anemones but broken wings

and blood wet feathers. I think of your ex
in North Carolina, how she might have perched

and looked out to razed earth, waiting for you
with your newly shaved beard, hand luggage

of notebooks and craft beer. Only for the fast
and brutal machine of my heart to catch you off guard.

Baggage

He texts again, calls himself *a train wreck*.
Last night he decapitated bottles of ale,
spent hours trying to find the perfect Rolex

to leave behind. He posts me tickets
to the Guns N' Roses gig we planned to go to,
says I can take my *new boyfriend or whatever*.

Wasn't he going to plant dahlias and watercress,
get in touch with old friends, give up
smoking, anime, video games?

He replies that he might go to Copenhagen,
visit a girl, sends pictures of her butterscotch lips,
the Hobbit ring he bought her for 700 quid,

the price of the rent I can barely scrimp together.
It's probably just sex or whatever, he says, wanting me
to imagine him pulling her hair, biting her neck.

My new love faces away from me like a tin
of baked beans he has turned so I can't see the calories.
Later he will remove all the grit from my coffee,

drive three-and-a-half hours to save me
the slight discomfort of a train. I wrap my arms
around him, buckle my legs at his waist.

My body, a rucksack I'm still trying to tear
the blades from to make space for journals
and lace underthings. All my reasons to recover.

It's 6.34 a.m. He texts, *There's nothing to live for.*
I am holding my new love thinking of buttered toast,
sliced hearts of grilled tomatoes.

Attendance Award

I willed away a flu, picked chickenpox off my skin,
held ice to my fevers, steam to my chills.

I'd have done anything for the award that declared
I was perfect, never slept in or missed a roll call,

a spelling test, a fire drill. Even now, outside
the GP's, my love holds open the door of his Ford

with the heat on full blast. He hands me a flask
of lemon and hibiscus tea. *Get in*, he says,

you're going to rest for the whole week,
his tone unkind, ungiving of choice,

knowing that to love me
means fighting another louder voice.

Marathon

Before we met I was on bed rest
for months, warned my heart would seize
if I ran, jogged, walked.

Still, I jumped jacks in the bathroom stall.
Maybe this is what it is to be in love,
to stand at the edge of a field, not doing

the thing my mind wills me to do
knowing that you're expecting me
with your sugar gels and Red Bull.

All the Things I Want to Do

I wake at six to sprint laps of the marina so I can eat
the rye toast you will grill for me later.

You hear me tighten my ponytail, knot the lace
of my shorts, my muscles tensed, facing away

from yours. You remind me of all the things
I want to do — parachute in Vancouver,

find the ring in a barmbrack. You laugh, say,
Even though you hate dried fruit. You plan a marathon

of movies, *Sister Act, The Rugrats,* a Sunday drive
to Lough Hyne. You suggest that some morning

we'll bake scones or soda bread. I reply
that I want *real* pancakes and my hand goes

to my lips to stuff back the words.
I never thought I would get to this stage,

sitting on the corner of your bed,
unclipping my sports bra, slipping off my ankle weights.

Mantras

Even with tea leaves of light
pouring through the window
my mind drags out the mantras —

DISCIPLINE IS DOING WHAT NEEDS TO BE DONE,
TODAY'S BRUISES ARE TOMORROW'S RESULTS.

There will always be this part of me
that wants to dress
in my old leotard of bone,

to hold closer than anything
belief in a future
where I could be perfect and loved.

Hiding

Mo chuisle holds a pillow over my face
    as a joke. This is how we love each other

knowing we can suffocate one another
    but won't. He wants me to get up,

eat sourdough with tapenade, climb Mizen Head
    to peer into the dark guts of the Atlantic,

hover our ankles over the 50-meter gorge.
    But I have ruined every cliff walk,

mountain trail by calculating how many steps
    I can take, how much I can burn.

It took so long to learn that I won't die
    if I sleep in or don't weigh the strain

I inflict on the earth. Now all I want is a life
    of shut curtains and holding the cracked teacup

of my body to his lips. The terrifying part is lifting
    the pillow, letting light back in.

Kinsale

Mostly I love you when I'm giving out
about the concrete garden of a single-storey house
where marigolds, foxgloves and asters

could shelter honeybees. A pond could refuge
natterjacks and newts, or an evergreen hold
red squirrels, the nest of a collared dove.

If we owned that bungalow I'd garnish our soup
with wild garlic, caramelize our onions,
honey-glaze fresh beets. Maybe we could raise

hens, quail or geese? Picture us waking up
to the kittiwake's song, a stroll from a port
where we greet by name the fishmonger,

dog walkers and rose-scented florist. How unfair
to be stuffed in an apartment we can't afford,
stacks of Tupperware leaning on cabinet doors.

You listen to me bark on and on like a city fox
before you reply that the slope from the porch
to the road looks fit for a wheelchair, fibromyalgia

or brittle bones. How can anything flourish or live
if we don't allow space for one another to grow?
My God, I'd create an Eden on our front lawn.

Acknowledgements and Notes

Acknowledgements are due to the editors of the following publications where some of these poems, or versions of them, were published first: *Anthropocene, Arena* (RTÉ) *Banshee, Cyphers, The Irish Times, Isolation Poetry Cards* (Dedalus Press), *One, Poetry Ireland Review, spoken worlds: southern syllables* (Ó Bhéal), *The Stinging Fly, This Is What You Mean To Me: Poetry Ireland Introductions 2021, Twin Skies* (Ó Bhéal Press, 2021) and *Washing Windows Too: Irish Women Write Poetry.*

'Crumbling' won the Padraic Colum Poetry Prize in 2019 and 'Under Your Skin' the Waterford Poetry Prize in 2020.

I would like to extend my sincerest thanks to Peter and Jean Fallon as well as Suella Holland of The Gallery Press for their knowledge, support and thoughtfulness. My gratitude to the Arts Council, ArtLinks, and Waterford Arts Office, in particular to Arts Officer Margaret Organ. I would also like to thank the team at Poetry Ireland, notably Elizabeth Mohen and Eoin Rogers. Acknowledgements are also due to the School of English in University College Cork, UCC Library, Cork City Library and the Tyrone Guthrie Centre.

For their wisdom and generosity, I am grateful to mentors Thomas McCarthy, Grace Wells, Dorianne Laux, Kevin Higgins, Leanne O'Sullivan and Sandra Beasley. Thanks are also due to Paul Casey and the folks at Ó Bhéal, Virginia Keane and the team at The Molly Keane Writers' Retreat, and Patrick Cotter and James O'Leary of the Munster Literature Centre. I am also thankful to Richard Krawiec of Jacar Press, Joanne McCarthy and Derek Flynn of The Waxed Lemon and Words Ireland for its mentorship programme.

Huge thanks are due to my poetry families at Ó Bhéal, the UCC MA class in Creative Writing from 2018/19, the Young Mystics poets and my Poetry Ireland Introductions peers from 2021.

Thanks are due to poets who have read my work and/or given me opportunities and support: Eoin Hegarty, Sonya Gildea, Simon Costello, John FitzGerald, Annemarie Ní Churreáin, Luke Morgan, Colm Keegan, Aoife Geraghty, Irene Long, Alison Mccrossan, Paddy Bushe and Beau Williams.

For her kindness, compassion and enduring friendship, my sincere thanks to my number one reader, Niamh Twomey. My deepest gratitude to Michael Ryan whose encouragement is integral to my recovery and ability to find joy in both life and writing.

A special thanks to my brothers, Paul and Michael Twomey, for their capacity to bring me warmth and laughter and for being empathetic and kind supporters of my writing. Gratitude is also due to my grandmother, Ann Twomey, for the way she can light up any room when she recites poetry and for allowing me to write in Inchera where a lot of this book was created. Thanks are also due to Fergal, Elva, Michael and Anne Twomey for letting me stay in their homes during writing programmes.

Finally, I would like to extend my deepest recognition and love to my parents Neil and Siobhán Twomey, whose strength and unwavering support has been crucial to the healing that enables me to write. None of this could happen without them.

> *page* 17   Mother 'threw anorexic daughter's body into the sea'. BBC News. BBC, 6 April 2017. https://www.bbc.com/news/world-europe-39511939